# Ants

## Melvin and Gilda Berger

**SCHOLASTIC INC.**
New York  Toronto  London  Auckland  Sydney
Mexico City  New Delhi  Hong Kong  Buenos Aires

**Photographs:** Cover: David T. Roberts/Photo Researchers; page 1: George Dodge/Bruce Coleman Inc.; page 3: Scott Camazine/Photo Researchers; page 4: Scott Camazine/Photo Researchers; page 5: Norman O. Tomalin/Bruce Coleman Inc.; page 6: Dr. Frieder Sauer/Okapia/Photo Researchers; page 7: Jeff Foott/Bruce Coleman Inc.; page 8: David T. Roberts/Photo Researchers; page 9: Bob Gossington/Bruce Coleman Inc.; page 10: K.G. Volk/Okapia/Photo Researchers; page 11: Rod Williams/Bruce Coleman Inc.; page 12: Gregory G. Dimijian/Photo Researchers; page 13: Gregory G. Dimijian/Photo Researchers; page 14: Gregory G. Dimijian/Photo Researchers; page 15: Norman Tomalin/Bruce Coleman Inc.; page 16: K.G. Vock/Photo Researchers.

ISBN 0-439-44537-X

12 11 10 9 8 7 6 5 4 3                    2 3 4 5 6 7/0

Printed in the U.S.A.
First Scholastic printing, September 2002

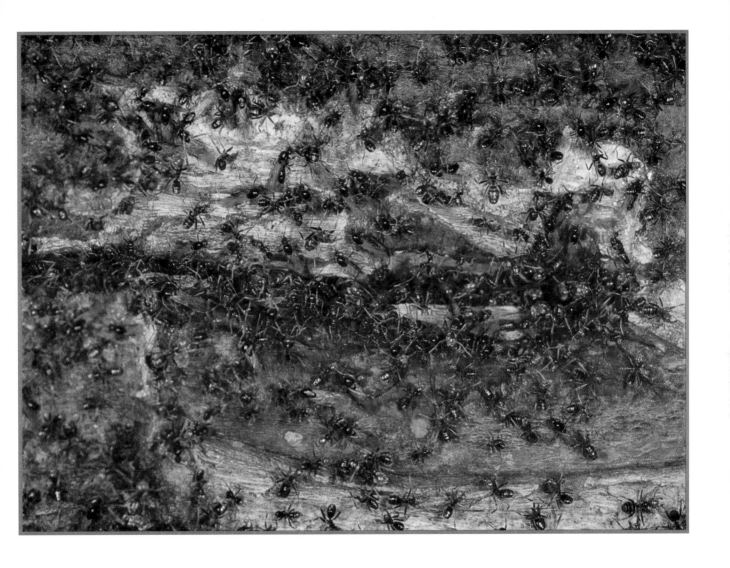

Ants live together.

**Fun Fact**
Most ant nests are under the ground.

Ants build nests — together.

Ants care for babies — together.

Ants find food — together.

Ants carry the food home —
together.

Ants grow from eggs — together.

**Fun Fact**

The queen ant lays all the eggs.

Ants care for eggs — together.

**Fun Fact**
Ants bite or sting when they fight.

Ants fight enemies — together.

Ants fight other ants — together.

Ants rest — together.

**Fun Fact**

Army ants travel in large groups and mainly attack other insects.

Many ants travel — together.

Ants can be very big.

Ants can be very small.

Big or small, ants do almost everything — together!